Awesome!

CUTE!

BOYS! BOYS! BOYS!

You ROCK!

SWEET!

I ♥ YOU

HE'S THE ONE!

© Parragon 2008 Pictures © Retna

First published in 2008 by Parragon

1 3 5 7 9 10 8 6 4 2

© Parragon 2008 Pictures © Retna

Printed and bound in China

CONTENTS

Total **HOTTIES**

ZAC EFRON

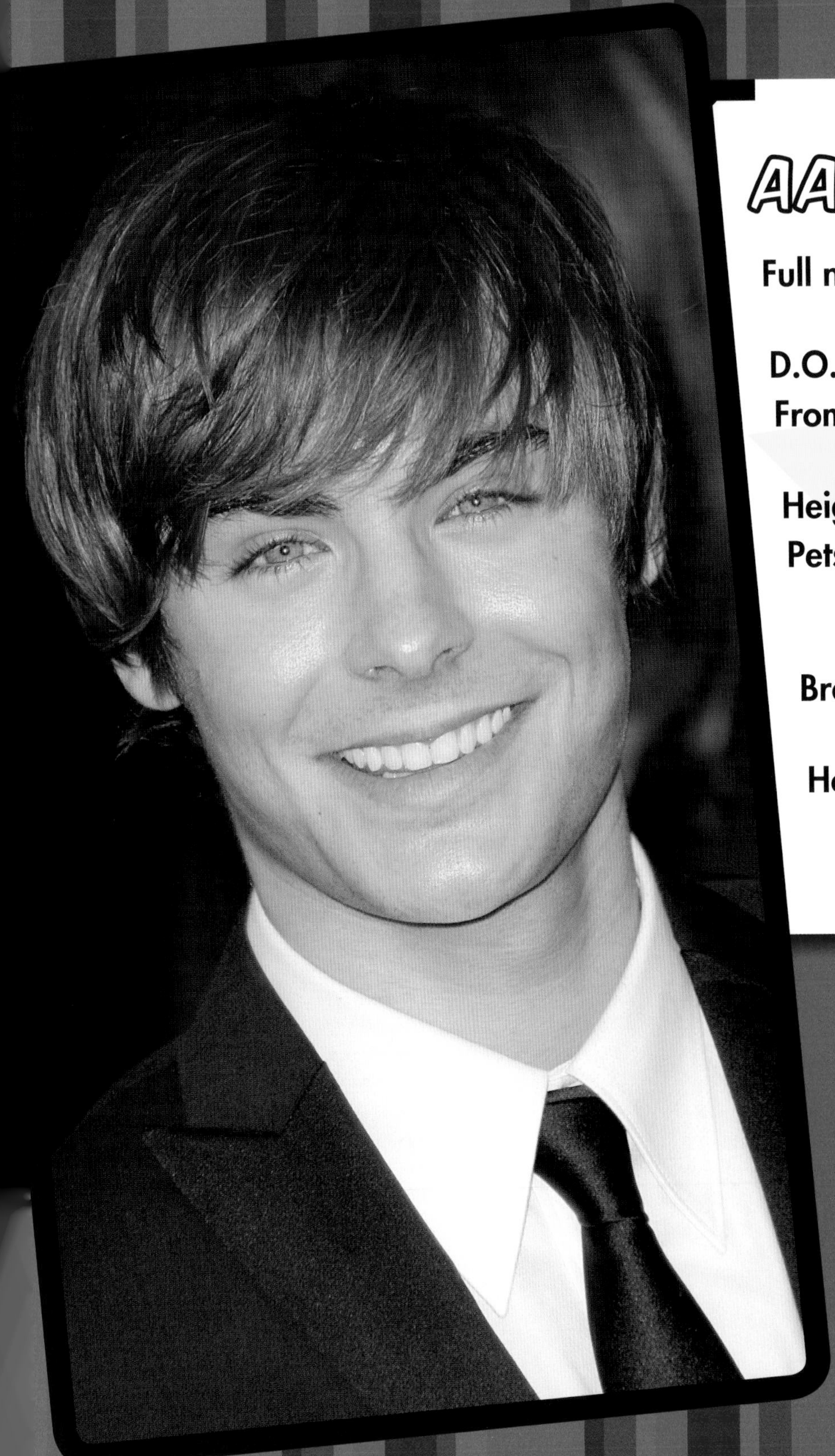

★ ★ ★ ★ ★ ★ ★ ★ ★ ★

AAA FACT FILE

Full name: Zachary David Alexander Efron

D.O.B: 18th October 1987

From: San Luis Obispo, California

Height: 5' 9" (1.75m)

Pets: Australian Shepherds, Dreamer and Puppy and Siamese cat, Simon

Bros/Sis: Younger brother, Dylan

Hobbies: Rock climbing, skiing and fixing up old cars

WHAT THEY SAY ABOUT ZE

Ashley Tisdale: "We're really close friends. He's like a brother to me – always there for me."

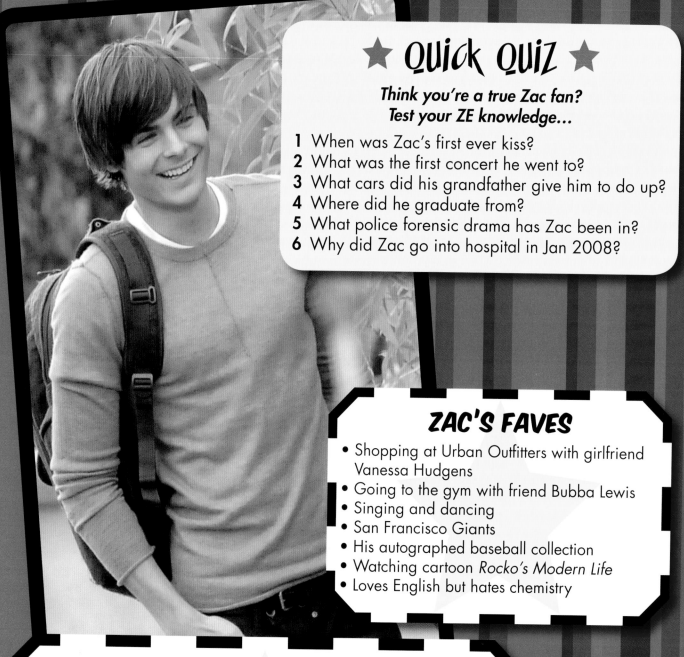

★ QUICK QUIZ ★

Think you're a true Zac fan?
Test your ZE knowledge…

1 When was Zac's first ever kiss?
2 What was the first concert he went to?
3 What cars did his grandfather give him to do up?
4 Where did he graduate from?
5 What police forensic drama has Zac been in?
6 Why did Zac go into hospital in Jan 2008?

ZAC'S FAVES

- Shopping at Urban Outfitters with girlfriend Vanessa Hudgens
- Going to the gym with friend Bubba Lewis
- Singing and dancing
- San Francisco Giants
- His autographed baseball collection
- Watching cartoon *Rocko's Modern Life*
- Loves English but hates chemistry

ZAC'S GUIDE TO LIFE

On asking someone out: "I think you need to find a place you're comfortable together and it will feel right to ask."
On being sensitive: "It's okay to cry – I always do when I watch Moulin Rouge!"
On helping others: "It's always good to give back. I regularly give to disadvantaged kids for the Toy Mountain Campaign."
On looking good: "I'm not a naturally groomed guy – I'm out the shower and ready to go in minutes"

Quiz Answers
1 Fifth grade in a tree house
2 Wallflowers
3 Delorean and '65 Mustang convertible
4 Arroyo Grande High School in June 2006
5 CSI: Miami
6 To have his appendix out

9

JESSE McCARTNEY

★ ★ ★ ★ ★ ★ ★ ★ ★ ★

AAA FACT FILE

Full name: Jesse Arthur McCartney

D.O.B: 9th April 1987

From: Ardsley, New York, USA

Height: 5' 9" (1.75m)

Pets: Cat named Oliver

Bros/Sis: Brothers Tim and Mark, sister Lea

Hobbies: Playing baseball, singing and acting

WHAT THEY SAY ABOUT JM

His keyboardist, Katie Spencer:
"I think that Jesse is very attractive but I don't see him anything more than a good friend."

★ QUICK QUIZ ★

Think you're a true Jesse fan? Test your JM knowledge...

1 What number in the US charts top 40 did Jesse's song "Beautiful Soul" make it to?
2 What UK singer songwriter from Southampton has influenced Jesse's music?
3 Do you know what Jesse has in common with Roger Daltrey and Christmas?
4 What pop star that sang "She Bangs" has collaborated with Jesse?
5 What was Jesse's first TV role?
6 Where did he graduate from?

JESSE'S FAVES

- Singing with Katie Cassidy
- Baseball and Football
- Snow/Water Skiing
- Actors Will Smith and Jim Carrey
- California Rolls and Pizza
- The colour orange
- Loves Maths and P.E.
- Hates history lessons

JESSE'S GUIDE TO LIFE

On girls: "Personality and a nice smile are the most important."
On the perfect date: "Go to the beach every time!"
On careers: "I honestly couldn't choose between acting and singing, so I try to balance both. It's important to sync all the things you want to do and just do them."
On handling success: "This is the best time of my life. I have so much support around me – my family, fans and management. It makes me want to work harder to make them proud."
On acting emotional scenes: "I always think of things that upset me a long time ago if I need to cry in a scene."

Quiz Answers
1 Number 3
2 Craig David
3 He starred with The Who rocker in A Christmas Carol when he was 10-years-old
4 Ricky Martin
5 Soap opera All My Children in 1998
6 Ardsley High School in Ardsley, New York

JUSTIN TIMBERLAKE

AAA FACT FILE

Full name: Justin Randall Timberlake

D.O.B: 31st January 1981

From: Memphis, Tennessee, USA

Height: 6' 1" (1.85m)

Pets: Two boxer dogs, Buckley and Brennen

Bros/Sis: Two half-brothers, Stephen and Jonathan

Hobbies: Golf and more golf

WHAT THEY SAY ABOUT JT

Madonna:
"I chose JT to honor my induction in to the Rock and Roll Hall of Fame because he's amazing, talented and cute."

★ QUICK QUIZ ★

Think you're a true Justin fan?
Test your JT knowledge…

1 What controversial "wardrobe malfunction" in 2004 did Justin cause at the Super Bowl?
2 Which famous mouse was Justin working with in 1996?
3 What men's fragrance company is Justin the face of?
4 Beside JC Chasez, who were Justin's other *NSYNC buddies?
5 What was Justin's first movie role and when was it?

JUSTIN'S FAVES

- Playing Scrabble
- Playing golf
- Watching movies
- Playing basketball
- Shopping
- The colour baby blue
- Playing video games

JUSTIN'S GUIDE TO LIFE

On singing: "Ever since I was a really little boy I always sang. So I figured that was sort of my calling. I didn't really have to think about it because I knew it was always there, that it's what I should be doing."
On playing games: "I do a lot of dinner parties and we play board games. I absolutely love Scrabble!"
On girls' smells: "It's really important that girls smell good; it makes them really attractive."
On his love: "Every relationship I've been in, I've overwhelmed the girl. They just can't handle all the love."
On gossip: "Gossip is called gossip because it's not always the truth."

Quiz Answers
1 He tore too much of Janet Jackson's costume off in the half-time show, revealing way too much!
2 He was a presenter, along with *NSYNC's JC Chasez, on Disney's The Mickey Mouse Club
3 Parfum Givenchy
4 Lance Bass, Joey Fatone and Chris Kirkpatrick
5 In the 1999 film Model Behavior

13

JAKE GYLLENHAAL

AAA FACT FILE

Full name: Jacob Benjamin Gyllenhaal

D.O.B: 19th December 1980

From: Los Angeles, California, USA

Height: 6' (1.83m)

Pets: Two dogs, a German shepherd called Atticus and a puggle, Boo Radley

Bros/Sis: Sister Maggie

Hobbies: Photography

WHAT THEY SAY ABOUT JG

Cyclist Lance Armstrong on Jake playing him in a movie of his life:

"You can't have a dude with his knees out here, head going back and forth... That's something I'll say about Jake: When he's riding, you think he's a bike rider, which is cool."

★ QUICK QUIZ ★

Think you're a true Jake fan?
Test your JG knowledge...

1 Which country is his family and ancestors from?
2 What film did Jake star in as a cowboy?
3 In which film did Jake almost get eaten by wolves and freeze to death?
3 What job at a swimming pool did Jake do when he was younger?
4 *Donnie Darko* was a cult hit film for Jake, but what year did it come out?
5 Who is Jake's godmother?

JAKE'S FAVES

- Going on vacation in Italy
- Getting involved in politics and world issues
- Dreaming he has the superpower of flying
- Shopping in SoHo
- Eating steak
- Riding his bike with friends Lance Armstrong and Matthew McConaughey
- Walking his dogs at Runyon Canyon, Hollywood
- Mario Batali's pizzas

JAKE'S GUIDE TO LIFE

On dealing with success: "It's funny to me that people find other people getting coffee really interesting, or walking their dog in the dog park."

On doing movies for a reason: "Aren't movies made to have something to say? Why make a movie if you don't have something to say? What are you doing it for?"

On love: "When two people love each other, they love each other. And people should hold on to it as hard as they can."

On life guarding: "I once helped someone who'd got stung by a man-o-war jellyfish by peeing on their leg. It helps stop the poison."

Quiz Answers
1 Sweden
2 *Brokeback Mountain*
3 The Day After Tomorrow
4 Lifeguard
5 2001
6 A. Jamie Lee Curtis

15

MILO VENTIMIGLIA

AAA FACT FILE

Full name: Milo Anthony Ventimiglia

D.O.B: 8th July 1977

From: Anaheim, California, USA

Height: 5' 10" (1.78m)

Pets: None

Bros/Sis: Two older sisters, Rose and Laurel

Hobbies: Restoring muscle cars made between 1964 and 1972

WHAT THEY SAY ABOUT MV

Heroes co-star Adrian Pasdar (who plays Milo's brother, Nathan Petrelli):

"I have a tremendous respect for Milo as a human being, and of course as an actor. We've become good friends over the course of this show."

⭐ QUICK QUIZ ⭐

Think you're a true Milo fan?
Test your M knowledge...

1 Where does Milo's last name come from?
2 Which hit TV comedy series did Milo star with Will Smith?
3 Which old British rock band does he love?
4 Milo is a lacto-vegetarian, but what does that mean?
5 Which theatre school did he attend?
6 How does Milo's character, Peter Petrelli, in *Heroes* differ from others with superpowers?

MILO'S FAVES

- Hanging out with co-star Hayden Panettiere at Hollywood's L Scorpion bar
- He hates drinking alcohol or smoking
- Snowboarding and skateboarding
- Driving his 1967 Chevelle he named Evelyn

MILO'S GUIDE TO LIFE

On having older sisters: "They used to dress me up as Madonna when I was younger. Don't ever let your sisters do that to you!"

On being whistled at in the street: "It's flattering, but it's hard for me to stomach the fact that people think I'm hot. To be honest, my nose is crooked from being broken so many times while wrestling. I don't seek attention. If anything, I'd rather blend in, remain anonymous."

On choosing your destiny: "If you want to be a positive, influential person, hang out with positive people. Adversely, if you want to walk a dark path, seek company with those that walk in the shadow."

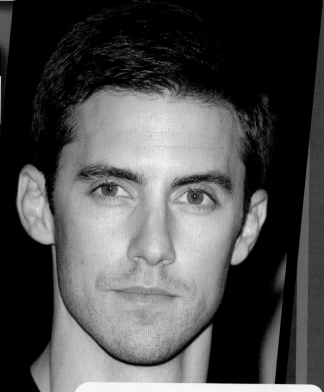

Quiz Answers

1 Ventimiglia is a town in Liguria, Italy
2 *The Fresh Prince of Bel Air*
3 The Clash
4 He doesn't eat meat but eats all dairy products except eggs
5 American Conservatory Theater in San Francisco, California
6 He can take on everyone's powers and use them all

ODD BODS
Guess these celebrity cuties by their body parts…

You'll find this English cutie in the Kingdom of Heaven…

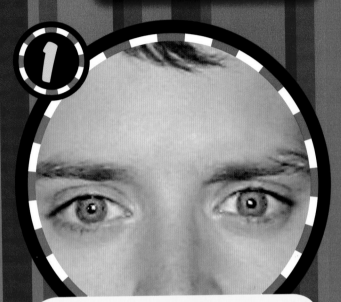

If you've ever lost a ring, then this guy is definitely the one to call to help you find it…

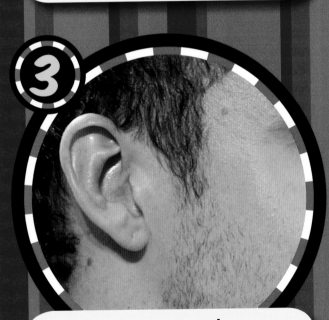

What time is it? It's time for this HSM hotster to reveal himself…

What goes around comes around for this singer/actor…

CELEBRITY SIDEKICKS

We love a boy who loves animals but what does their pet choice say about them?

Judge for yourself below as we take a look at which animal is your favourite boys' latest squeeze **WOOF!**

66 *Oh, sometimes he's a bit odd with other dogs... I got him in a Moroccan street market.* **99**

66 *My dogs are crazy. They're always getting into some kind of trouble... but then again, they're my most loyal friends.* **99**

SAY WHAT?

Match the quote to the celeb and see just how celeb-mad you really are!

1. Which soul-boy said:

" ...If I see a room full of girls, I'm gonna go in and be like 'hey, how y'all doing?' and just chill with them!... "

a Chris Brown
b Nick Jonas
c Pete Wentz

2. Name this actor:

" ...I'm certain I'm going to fail as an actor, so I better have something else to do... "

a Justin Timberlake
b Ashton Kutcher
c Matt Damon

3. Name the rock boy who said:

" ...We hung out with Good Charlotte's Joel Madden – he's the biggest celebrity we've ever met!... "

a Nick Jonas
b Pierre Bouvier, Simple Plan
c Gerard Way, MCR

4. Which actor gushed:

"*...Kissing Rachel (Bilson) was one of the best kisses. She's a pretty girl and a sweetheart...*"
a Hayden Christensen
b Adam Brody
c Ben McKenzie

5. Which A-lister said:

"*...I love my dog, I love my dog so much, more than anything in the world...*"
a Ben Affleck
b Orlando Bloom
c Brad Pitt

6. Which musician said:

"*...My worst habit? Picking fluff out my belly button and burping...*"
a Justin Timberlake
b Brandon Flowers
c Jared Leto

Answers
1 a Chris Brown 2 b Ashton Kutcher 3 b Pierre Bouvier 4 a Hayden Christensen 5 b Orlando Bloom 6 a Justin Timberlake

Total
HOTTIES

PUCKER UP WITH
CORBIN BLEU

★ ★ ★ ★ ★ ★ ★ ★ ★ ★ ★ ★

Pssst! Wanna find out some sizzlin' smoochin' secrets from High School Musical star, Corbin Bleu? Pucker up for the hottest tips straight from his lush lips. Mwoaaah!

HIS ULTIMATE DATE...

Seems Corbin is quite the romantic and likes nothing more than to make the girl he's with feel super special.
"A hand in hand walk on the beach and a candlelit dinner really appeals to me."

THE BEST WAY TO ATTACT ATTENTION...

If you want to catch Corbin' eye, you have to stand out from the crowd.
"When a girl walks into a room and you can sense there's something special about her, that's what I like."

THE KIND OF GIRL WHO ROCKS HIS WORLD...

Corbin is a sucker for a great personality and loves a girl he can have a good conversation with.
"I'm not a shy person and, when I hang out with you, I want to be able to talk to you. I'm quite outgoing so I like a girl who isn't afraid to be herself."

KISSING - EYES OPEN OR CLOSED?

Corbin's a close-your-eyes-when-you-smooch kind of guy, but he says it really depends on the kiss.
"If it feels right to keep them open, then open them up. And if it feels right to keep them closed, just shut them!"

KISS AND TELL TIPS

Brush up – This one is obvious, but make sure you always brush your teeth to keep them clean, and maybe have gum or mints handy in case you're going to have a kiss. Get some nice, minty gum to chew on pre-kiss – that's always good! Oh, and avoid garlic at all costs!

Take it slow – Go easy and take your time. The best kisses happen when things are taken nice and slow. Make sure you're both ready – if it doesn't feel right, don't do it.

Enjoy – Kisses are very special and it's easy to get nervous about them. The best piece of advice is to enjoy it. Have fun.

25

LIGHTS, CAMERA
ACTION!

★ ★ ★ ★ ★ ★ ★ ★ ★ ★ ★

We love nothing more than a trip to the movies to watch our favourite hotsters in action on the big screen. These are our favourite scene-stealing moments!

HSM

We love it when Troy sings with Gabriella for the first time in *HSM*! He discovers he's good at something other than basketball and falls head over heels in love with Gabriella at the same time… *Sigh!*

HAIRSPRAY

Who wouldn't ♥ Link when he's singing into a hairbrush and declaring love for Tracy Turnblad – we just wish he was declaring love to us!

JUMP IN

Corbin Bleu is hot-to-trot especially when skipping Double Dutch! Our favourite scene? When Corbin's character Izzy arrives at the tournament and says "What, were you really gonna start without me?" *Go, Izzy, go!*

HARRY POTTER

Harry Potter hotty, Daniel Radcliffe took thirty takes to get his first screen kiss right in the film *Order of the Phoenix.*

Daniel said: "We probably got it on the 30th take. My god it was fun. Me and Katie - we were awkward and nervous at first but once we got it, it was fine." What we wouldn't give to be this wizard's leading lady!

HOORAY FOR
HSM

★ ★ ★ ★

Find words from the feel-good hit hidden in the grid!

★ Musical ★ Troy ★ Gabriella ★ Sharpay ★

East High ★ Dancing ★ Singing ★ Fabulous

M	G	A	B	R	I	E	L	L	A
S	U	O	L	U	B	A	F	T	P
D	S	S	I	N	G	I	N	G	R
S	H	G	I	H	T	S	A	E	Y
H	A	G	H	C	A	B	U	O	P
A	R	G	N	M	A	O	U	A	D
R	P	E	O	Y	O	L	V	I	L
D	A	N	C	I	N	G	O	L	A
S	Y	O	R	T	P	L	Z	A	N
L	O	I	B	V	E	T	H	A	B

CORBIN BLUE

WALL CANDY

DOUBLE TROUBLE

Born 15 minutes apart, the Sprouse twins, the super-cute boys from The Suite Life of Zack & Cody are as close as brothers get – but what sets Dylan and Cole apart?

Who's the elder one?

Dylan was an only child for a whole 15 minutes before Cole came on the scene!

What about falling out?

These two are typical siblings and fight over weird little things like who got the last scoop of ice cream or who called the last muffin!

But no big bust-ups, then?

One time, they had a fight in their dressing room – they were wrestling on the floor when an extra came in and asked for a photo mid-punch!

A secret we don't know about the boys is...

That they're big nerds! They like things like Godzilla and comics – nerd boys rule!

Wanna date Cole and Dylan?

Good news they're both single! Cole likes girls he can relate to – girls who are funny, outgoing and want to have fun, while Dylan wants a girl who isn't star struck, so no "oh gosh! You're Zack and Cody!"

SPROUSE FAVOURITES

	Dylan Vs Cole	
Subject	Science	Maths
Pizza topping	Pepperoni	Bacon bits
Reality show	*Fear Factor*	*Super Nanny*
Sport	Surfing	Snowboarding
Animal	Wolf	Pig

ROAD TO SUCCESS

JOSH HARTNETT

Born in San Francisco on July 21 1978

Got his first stage roles when he was a little boy in Minneapolis, which included *Tom Sawyer* at the Children's Theater Company and *Freedom Riders* at the Youth Performance Center

In 1996, after graduating, Josh joined the acting program at SUNY Purchase, New York. That didn't last as he was kicked out for slacking!

Grew up in St. Paul, Minnesota

ASHTON KUTCHER

Went to Washington High School in Cedar Rapids before doing lots of outdoor cowboy-type jobs such as carpentry, hay-baling and herding cattle.

In 1998 he moved to LA and was cast as Michael Kelso in the television series *That '70s Show*, which started its run in 1998 and ended in 2006.

Born in Cedar Rapids, Iowa on February 7 1978

At 13 he moved to Tiffin, Iowa where he attended the Clear Creek-Amana High School.

MARK WAHLBERG

Went to Copley Square High School in Boston but flunked out.

Born in Dorchester, Boston, Massachusetts on June 5 1971.

In 1992 he started modelling underwear for Calvin Klein and a billboard in New York's Times Square featured a massive poster of him.

In 1997 he moved to LA for TV acting work and got his first role on the hard-hitting ABC drama, *Cracker*. This role was Josh's breakthrough performance. It really fired him into the stratosphere.

In 2004 he starred with Scarlett Johansson in *The Black Dahlia*, a dark crime thriller set in Los Angeles.

In 2008 he played Tom in the film *August* – a touching movie about two brothers working in New York around the time of 9/11.

In 2006 he starred in *30 Days of Night*.

In 2002 he briefly went back to his birthplace San Francisco to film rom-com *40 Days and 40 Nights* where he starred as Matt Sullivan.

In 2000 he was in road trip comedy *Dude, Where's My Car?*

In 2005 he became an executive producer of the reality TV show *Beauty and the Geek* and also married actress Demi Moore this year too.

In 2008 he starred opposite Cameron Diaz in Las Vegas rom-com *What Happens in Vegas...*

In 2001 he lost out after an audition to be Danny Walker in *Pearl Harbor* to Josh Hartnett. Boo!

In 2008 he was in scary blockbuster *The Happening*.

In 2001 he bought a $5 million dollar mansion in Beverly Hills.

In 2004 he became executive producer on the hit TV series about celebrity hotties partying all day and night in Hollywood, *Entourage*.

At the moment he's reportedly working on a follow-up to *The Departed*.

ZAC V CORBIN

They may appear in the same feel-good smash HSM, but these best buds couldn't be more different... go compare!

Personality: Zac is bright, breezy and takes things as they come. He's light-hearted, always smiling and up for a laugh, looks up to icons like Elvis and is a bundle of energy 24/7.

Style: Zac loves to shop, especially at Urban Outfitters, and usually works a casual smart but always funky look – swoon.

Friends: He has a gaggle of gal pals including all the Hollywood sparkly ones like Ashley Tisdale and Vanessa Hudgens – he also loves to hang with his best gym-going buddy, Bubba Lewis.

ZAC

Star Sign: Libra

Music: It's no wonder Zac has appeared in both *HSM* and *Hairspray* this guy loves, loves, loves the musicals, especially old ones from the 60's.

Personality: Corbin is a thinker and takes acting very seriously, don't worry though this deep and meaningful dude is also able to flick his happy switch to reveal that award winning grin of his!

Style: This guy knows how to dress and is most relaxed kicking back in urban, funky cool – y'dig?!

Friends: He has gal-pals too, in fact his bestest pal is Monique Coleman! He also loves to hang with his three sisters too – what a cool bro!

Star Sign: Pisces

Music: Corbin likes his tunes chilled, and loves to mix up his own block-rockin' beats. His favourite musical era is definitely the 80s – just as long as he doesn't start looking there for fashion inspiration – he'll keep his cool kid crown!

CORBIN

WE ♥ JOHNNY

REASONS WHY MR. DEPP'S AS SWEET AS CHOCOLATE...

HE'S MODEST!

He claims he was surprised he was chosen to play Willy Wonka. "I know there were a couple of big names (up for the part) so I felt they were going to go for a big star." Er, hello, you are a big star, J!

HE ROCKS!

Johnny didn't plan to be an actor – he fronted a lot of different guitar bands in his teens 'cause he wanted to be a rock star!

HE'S SWEET

He reckons his character Willy Wonka in *Charlie and the Chocolate Factory* was a bit lonely, which explains why he behaves so strangely. Johnny decided he wanted to show him as a sensitive type despite all his weird ways…

HE'S GORGEOUS!

Okay, so he might be getting on a bit, but Johnny's still a major-league cutie. No wonder the ladies love him so much. He's been engaged three times and married once – but he's now with French girlfriend, Vanessa Paradis and they have two children together, son Jack and daughter Lily Rose.

WEIRD OR WHAT?

⭐ Johnny absolutely loves sticky toffee pudding. In fact he says he's addicted to it!

⭐ He nicknamed himself "Mr. Stench" and used to think it was funny to check into hotels using his fake name.

⭐ His surname Depp means "twit" in German!

⭐ He's not keen on dentists – which is why he kept the gold caps on his teeth for ages after filming *Pirates of the Caribbean*!

⭐ He likes playing with Barbie dolls!

WHAT THEY GO TO SCHOOL FOR

See if you can match these stars to their class memories…

"…I was a nerd. I had no friends and I got picked on because I didn't have a lot of money…"

1.....................................

"When I got in trouble at school I would have loved to have taken an invisible cloak, drape it over me and sneak out the door…"

2.....................................

"…I was the class clown, it was fun!"

3.....................................

"…I didn't get into trouble for doing naughty things. I was just a bit lazy and couldn't be bothered to do my homework. Sometimes I'd get told off for not being able to stop giggling in classes!"

4.....................................

"…Out of all my dancing classes, I was quite good at tap. It's funny, coz I used to do ballet too. I bet there's some really bad pictures of me wearing ballet shoes!"

5.....................................

A

B

C

D

E

BOYS WITH GUITARS

Get ready to rock, girls! We've got the lowdown on some of the hottest boys who will rock and rule your world!

THE JONAS BROTHERS

The Jonas Brothers are a super cute American pop-punk/pop-rock band from Wyckoff, New Jersey made up of three brothers, Joseph, Nicholas and Kevin Jonas. They've released two albums – *It's About Time* and the self-titled *Jonas Brothers*, toured with pop princesses, *Hannah Montana* and Avril Lavigne and star in the Disney Channel's fabulous TV movie *Camp Rock*.

WHY YOU'LL LOVE THEM:

They're easy-on-the-eye and make the catchiest music you'll ever hear - we heart Jonas Brothers!

KEEPING IT SIMPLE

Our plan is definitely simple, we want to date **PIERRE BOUVIER!**

Pierre is one-third of the Montreal-based punk-pop group Simple Plan, which is comprised of high school pals Pierre Bouvier, (vocals – we can't help thinking he's singing his songs just for us – sigh.), Jeff Stinco (guitar), David Desrosiers (bass), Sebastien Lefebvre (guitar), and Chuck Comeau (drums).

WE ASKED PIERRE, WHEN'S THE LAST TIME YOU...

Chatted with a celebrity? "We toured with Good Charlotte recently, and I hung out with Joel Madden. He's a good guy. He's always on the cover of magazines with Nicole Richie, so he counts as a big celebrity!"

Read an untrue story about yourself? All the time, and none of it is ever true! The last story I read was that David, our guitarist, and me were a couple. People make up some crazy stuff."

Kissed a girl? "That would be my mum. I kissed her goodbye before we set off on tour – just a peck on the cheek."

Went to a good party? "We have cool after show parties after our gigs, but we can never stay for very long 'cause we have to get up early to catch a flight to our next concert."

Caught up with the gossip on a blog? "I read Perez Hilton's page regularly. He seems to like us, so never writes any bad stuff about us on his website. He's got a small part in our video for *When I'm Gone*. Look out for him!

FAST FACTS ON MY CHEMICAL ROMANCE

We bring you up to speed on the New Jersey rockers...

1. The lads have already sold over one million records world wide.
2. They played two shows in one day at London's Astoria, complete with a Victorian funeral procession that stopped the traffic outside!
3. Singer Gerard Way and bassist Mikey Way are brothers.
4. They've toured the USA with the amazing Green Day.
5. On stage they wear bullet-proof vests.
6. Plastic fantastic! They've just had action figures made of themselves.
7. The boys are American but made it big in the UK first.
8. Gerard's also a talented artist – he designs all the covers for the band's CDs.
9. While filming *The Ghost of You* vid on a boat, the lads had a narrow escape when it started to sink!
10. All the videos have reached the No1 spot on MTVs TRL show!

30 SECONDS WITH JARED

Not only is Jared Leto a Hollywood A-lister – he fronts the very cute-to-look-at rock band 30 Seconds to Mars. From movie-star-boy-next-door to Emo screamer – here's Jared's career in brief!

- Jaz started out as eye candy opposite a young-looking Claire Danes in the American TV series *My So-Called Life*
- He then moved on to films including *The Thin Red Line*, *Urban Legend*, *Fight Club* and *Panic Room*
- Yes, it's Jared under all that hair – he starred with Winona Ryder and Angelina Jolie in *Girl, Interrupted*
- Our boy with his band – guitarist Tomo Milicevic and drummer Shannon Leto, Jared's big bro!

ARE YOU WITH THE BAND?

★ BAND TEASER ★

Match each band member of
The Killers to the trivia about him

1. _____ formed the band by placing an ad in a paper

2. _____ has a phobia of the number 62!

3. _____ is half Italian and half German

4. _____ has the middle name August

Answers: Dave Keuning Brandon Flowers Ronnie Vannucci Jr. Mark Stoermer

CELEB SECRET

Which Brit rock band named themselves after a South African footie team?

A. Kaiser Chiefs

★ BAND TEASER ★

Can you mention each member of The Cribs to a statement?

1. _____ has worked for a vet and in a toilet roll factory

2. _____ reckons he'd do woodwork if the band failed

3. _____ ended up in hospital after falling on a huge jar of sweets at an award ceremony!

GUESS WHO?
Use the facts to find the celeb

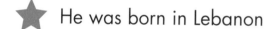

★ He was born in Lebanon

★ His surname is Penniman

★ He's been trained as an opera singer

★ He thinks big girls are beautiful!

★ He once wrote a jingle for Orbit chewing gum

ZAC EFRON

WALL
CANDY

I'M WITH THE BAND!

So you think you're Nick, Joe and Kevin's biggest fan?
Test your Jonas Brothers knowledge here...

1. Which Jonas brother was born on 5th November 1987?

2. What Jonas Bother sings lead vocal?

3. Which role does Nick Jonas play in the movie *Camp Rock*?

4. Which skater girl did the Jonas Brothers tour with in 2008?

Answers: 1 – Kevin, 2 – Nick,
3 – Nate, 4 – Avril Lavigne,

Name that song! Which Jonas Brother tracks do the following lyrics come from?

5. "...One day when I came home at lunchtime, I heard a funny noise..."

6. "...I know we get a little crazy, I know we get a little loud, I know we're never gonna fake it..."

Answers: 5 – Year 3000,
6 – That's just the way we roll,

WHO'S BODY PARTS ARE THESE?

Answers: 7 – Joe, 8 – Nick 9 – Kevin

NAME THE AIR GUITARIST

Answers: 10 – Joe, 11 – Kevin 12 – Nick

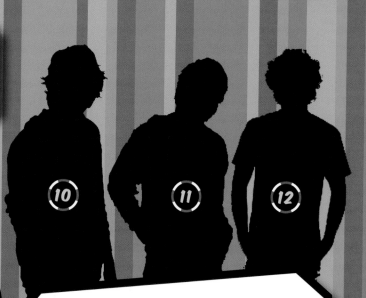

FANTASY LINE UP

Wouldn't it be awesome if all your favourite muso-boys were in one band? Decide who'd be in musical dream team from these gorgeous choices...

★ ★ ★ ★ ★ ★ ★ ★ ★ ★

LEAD SINGERS

They've got a killer voice and can make any lyric sound amazing!

Gerard Way, My Chemical Romance

✔ – Has amazing stage presence and could totally teach you how to do your make-up.

✘ – He's intense – sometimes maybe a little too intense.

Joel Madden, Good Charlotte

✔ – Has a rags-to-riches story we just love and looks great on stage.

✘ – He's dating Nicole Richie.

Jared Leto, 30 Seconds to Mars

✔ – He's so very, very pretty. Sigh.

✘ – Is happy to wear his guy-liner to the supermarket, in fact, he's hardly seen without it – guys in make-up are cute, but not when they wear more than you!

LEAD GUITAR

Second-in-command and usually really rather cute – it must come with the guitar lessons!

Jeff Stinco, Simple Plan

✔ – Great sense of humour.

✘ – You would need patience – it's taken them ages to come up with a third album, would hate him to keep us waiting that long on a date!

Nathan Connolly, Snow Patrol

✔ – He can do double duty as a back-up vocalist.

✘ – Has an almost unhealthy obsession with the movie Star Wars.

Joe King, The Fray

✔ – Hard-working and never expected overnight success.

✘ – He considered switching from a music career to one in property – yawnsville.

BASSIST

These guys are the backbone to the band, helping to keep rhythm and time, not to mention they add funk!

Pete Wentz, Fall Out Boy

✔ – He is easy on the eye and writes catchy sing-a-long-to songs.

✘ – He's a mummy's boy. "… my mom doesn't like the songs that are about hating people. Anything about hating, she won't listen to"

Jason McCaslin, Sum 41

✔ – Love that he got his nickname "Cone", from eating ice cream cones all the time.

✘ – Last member to join, so has had less time in the band.

Mikey Way, My Chemical Romance

✔ – Rumour has it, that Mickey learned bass just so he could be a member of MCR!

✘ – Left MCR briefly to deal with personal problems.

DRUMS

They keep the rhythm of the whole band – one false move and everyone would be thrown off. It's a tough job being a drummer y'know!

Spencer Smith, PANIC! at the DISCO

✔ – Begged his parents for a drum set so he could rock out with neighbour (and future band mate) Ryan Ross.

✘ – Actually we can't really think of one, he's fab!

Tre Cool, Green Day

✔ – Is an industry veteran, making him the most experienced drummer of the lot.

✘ – He's so quiet in interviews you wouldn't know he was there.

Chuck Comeau, Simple Plan

✔ – Not afraid to take the lead during interviews.

✘ – Has a bit of a slacker reputation.

READY TO ROCK?

Crazy about celeb-boys with guitars? Or do they just drive you mad? Find out here...

1. Where was Jared Leto born?

A Louisiana

B Haiti

C New York

2. Which of these boys isn't in Simple Plan?

A Jeff Stinco

B David Desrosiers

C Travis Parker

3. What's the name of Green Day's pop-eyed singer?

A Billy Joel

B Billie Jean

C Billy Joe

4. Which country do the Rasmus come from?

A Finland

B Sweden

C Lapland

5. Where did the group Franz Ferdinand get together?

A Glasgow

B Hemel Hempstead

C Surbiton

6. Which role did Marilyn Manson play in the film version of Alice in Wonderland?

A The Mad Hatter

B The Queen of Hearts

C The Cheshire Cat

7. Finish off the name of this Zutons' track: Don't Ever Think...

A (About Boys)

B (It's Over)

C (Too Much)

8. What are the names of the twin brothers in Good Charlotte?

A Bill and Ben

B Jim and Jon

C Benji and Joel

9. Which TV show have Blink 182 starred in?

A The X Factor

B Holby City

C Laguna Beach: The Real OC

10. Where did "Panic!" At The Disco get their name from?

A A song called Panic by The Smiths

B They were scared at their local disco once

C They get panicked when they play live

7 – 10 points: Rock Goddess

Wow girl, we salute you! Is there anything you don't know about the extra-loud boys of rock? You sure you know your Bowling For Soup from your New Found Glory. Have you ever thought of starting a band? We reckon you'd be right at home strutting your stuff in front of the mosh pit – or just having a laugh with your air guitar! Go to the top of the rock class...

4-6 points: Halfway Honey

Okay, so you're not into the hardcore sounds of guitar boys – but hey, it takes all sorts. You love Blink 182 and while the heavier stuff like The Rasmus or Good Charlotte might not be your thing, 30 seconds from Mars are right up your street – plus they look cute. Maybe you should try listening to something tougher – give The Zutons a go. We reckon you'll love 'em...

0-3 points: Pop Princess

Umm...do you know what a guitar is? You may love your R&B and disco stuff, but why not give the boys of rock a go? What about The Strokes? They're cooler than cool and you can dance to them. Be adventurous – you can't shimmy to rock but you can jump up and down to it. Which is even more fun sometimes!

Answers: 1 – A, 2 – C, 3 – C, 4 – A, 5 – A, 6 – B, 7 – C, 8 – C, 9 – C, 10 – A

WALL CANDY

DESTINY DATES

CRACK YOUR COLOUR CODE

Find out what your favourite shade reveals about you and who your celeb colour companion *really* is!

PINK...

You're an optimist and view the world through rose-tinted glasses. You always try and see the good in people and make the best of any situation, however tricky. Proud to be girlie, you're a sucker for all things pink, from hair straighteners to MP3 players.

Your colour code partner is: Zac Efron

Zac is totally in touch with his girlie side and isn't afraid to cry at the movies. All together now... awwww!

RED...

You ooze charisma and confidence. You love to boss your mates about and they'll do as you say 'cause they think you rock! You love fashion and are a real trend-setter. You can be quite stubborn, though and find it hard to apologize even when you need to.

Your colour code partner is: Justin Timberlake

You both know how to grab attention and heads would definitely turn if you and Justin were to walk in a room!

GREEN...

If your mates are squabbling, you'll be the one to step in and sort it out. You're super organized and hate it when people are late – but some people can find your perfectionist streak a bit irritating. Try to relax and let your hair down once in a while.

Your colour code partner is: Corbin Bleu

If Corbin is anything like his character in HSM, he'll be hugely protective of you and will step up to make sure everyone gets on – our hero!

BLUE...

You're caring and loyal, and love your family and friends more than anything. Your mates confide you in you 'cause they know you can keep a secret. But be careful certain people don't take advantage of your good nature. You can be quite shy and quiet and prefer going to the cinema than a loud party.

Your colour code partner is: Jake Gyllenhaal

This super-cute geek boy is totally adorable, loves his family and would be the perfect boy to curl up with on your sofa and watch a film together!

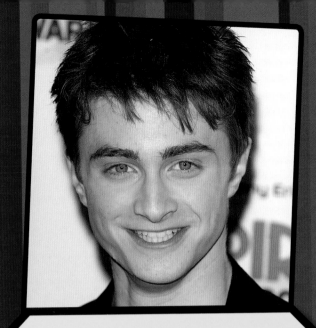

ORANGE...

Everyone likes you and wants to hang out with you 'cause you're so friendly and sociable. You love chatting to your mates about anything from clothes to your crush – just be careful that you don't overspend on your mobile bill. Sometimes you're so desperate to avoid hurting people's feelings that you're too nice for your own good.

Your colour code partner is: Adam Brody

He is the most likeable boy on screen, he has lots of cute mates and loves to talk – match made in heaven!

YELLOW...

You love learning and trying out new stuff, from modern dance to martial arts. You have loads of mates and find it hard to say no to them when they ask you for favours. Just make sure that every once in a while, you take time out to treat yourself too.

Your colour code partner is: Daniel Radcliffe

Daniel, not content with being in the most successful movie ever, is now trying his hand at theatre and TV presenting – he's super popular and a date with him would be guaranteed to be magical!

WHAT'S HE LIKE?

Use the stars to suss out which
star-boy you should date...

ARIES

Always enthusiastic, he is usually the first one to suggest a good night out. He's seen as the wild one of the bunch – which means he can be a bit over the top at times. And as a natural leader, he's a bit bossy, too. But you can count on him to stick up for you.

Aries dates: Ewan McGregor, Zach Braff

TAURUS

Taureans make very faithful and grounded hang-out buds, although they do tend to sulk when they're not getting enough attention. A Taurean can also be stubborn and won't give up easily. He's usually very determined and just oozes ambition, which is a great vibe to be around.

Taurus date: David Beckham

GEMINI

A real spark of the zodiac, Gemini's love the sound of their own voices! They enjoy a good gossip too, and you'll always catch them trying to juggle about a hundred things at once. Gemini boys get bored easily so don't suggest doing the same thing to him two weekends in a row.

Gemini dates: Johnny Depp, Kanye West, Ashton Kutcher

CANCER

Cancerians love their home surroundings. So he'd be more likely to suggest going over his place to watch DVDs rather than hitting the town. He's sometimes hard to get close to, but once you make the effort, you'll gain his trust for life.

**Cancer dates:
Daniel Radcliffe,
50 Cent, Josh Hartnett,
Milo Ventimiglia**

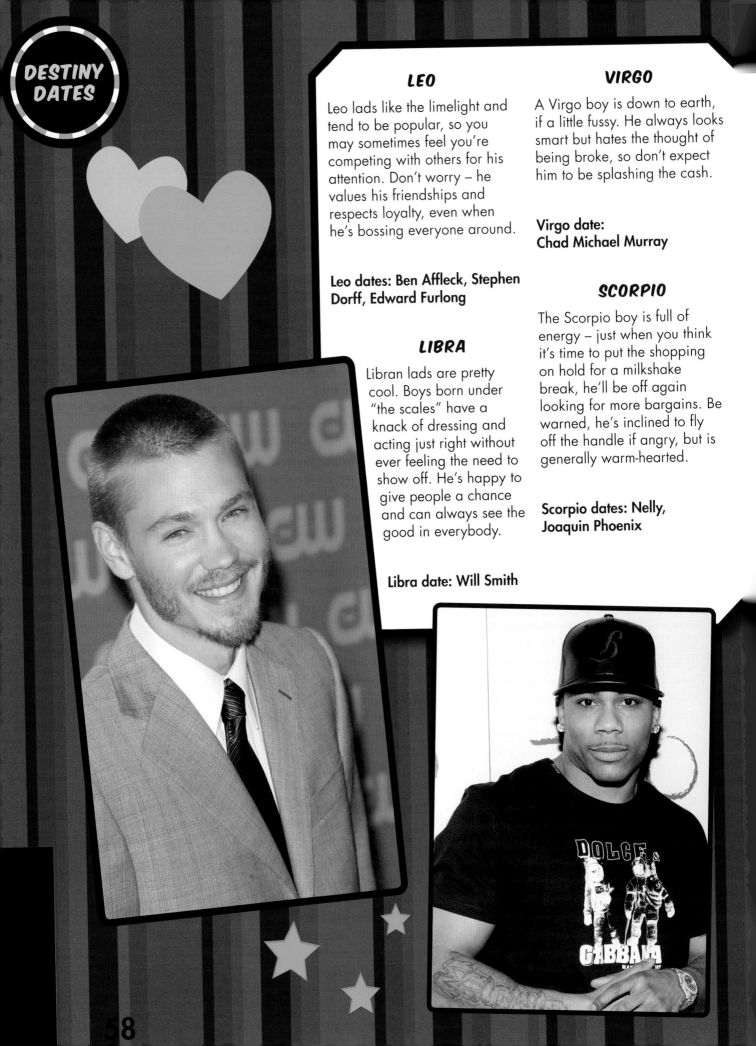

LEO

Leo lads like the limelight and tend to be popular, so you may sometimes feel you're competing with others for his attention. Don't worry – he values his friendships and respects loyalty, even when he's bossing everyone around.

Leo dates: Ben Affleck, Stephen Dorff, Edward Furlong

LIBRA

Libran lads are pretty cool. Boys born under "the scales" have a knack of dressing and acting just right without ever feeling the need to show off. He's happy to give people a chance and can always see the good in everybody.

Libra date: Will Smith

VIRGO

A Virgo boy is down to earth, if a little fussy. He always looks smart but hates the thought of being broke, so don't expect him to be splashing the cash.

**Virgo date:
Chad Michael Murray**

SCORPIO

The Scorpio boy is full of energy – just when you think it's time to put the shopping on hold for a milkshake break, he'll be off again looking for more bargains. Be warned, he's inclined to fly off the handle if angry, but is generally warm-hearted.

Scorpio dates: Nelly, Joaquin Phoenix

SAGITTARIUS

Sagittarians have a knack of being able to see three different friends at three different places in one day, so try not to get too offended when they have to dart off. They're always on the go as they like to keep busy and love surrounding themselves with a big crowd of people.

Sagittarius dates: Jesse Metcalfe, Jake Gyllenhaal

CAPRICORN

Capricorns are very wise and can seem more mature than they really are, but that doesn't mean they don't enjoy having fun. They have a brilliant sense of loyalty too, so make sure you hold on to him.

Capricorn dates: Jared Leto, Orlando Bloom, Jude Law

AQUARIUS

Even though he may appear to be distant or aloof at times, Aquarian boys don't mean to act cold. They like their own space or hanging out with close friends. And they love discovering new things, so don't be surprised if he's the first to get the latest gadgets – in fact, he's probably had an ipod before the rest of us knew what they were.

Aquarius date: Justin Timberlake

PISCES

When it comes to having fun, a Pisces boy is probably first on the dance floor and the last to leave at the end of the night. They're not hardcore partygoers, but they do love to boogie. The rest of the time, these romantic souls are usually lost in a bit of a dream world!

Pisces dates: Benji - Good Charlotte, Jesse McCartney

STARS GET SLOPPY
These celeb lads talk love, crushes and snogs...

"*I'm a hopeless romantic and I love to spoil my girlfriends, but my first kiss was a disaster. I didn't know what to say before I kissed her, so I came out with 'Can I get off with you?' I was only nine and she slapped my face. I hope she's forgiven me now.*"

Orlando Bloom

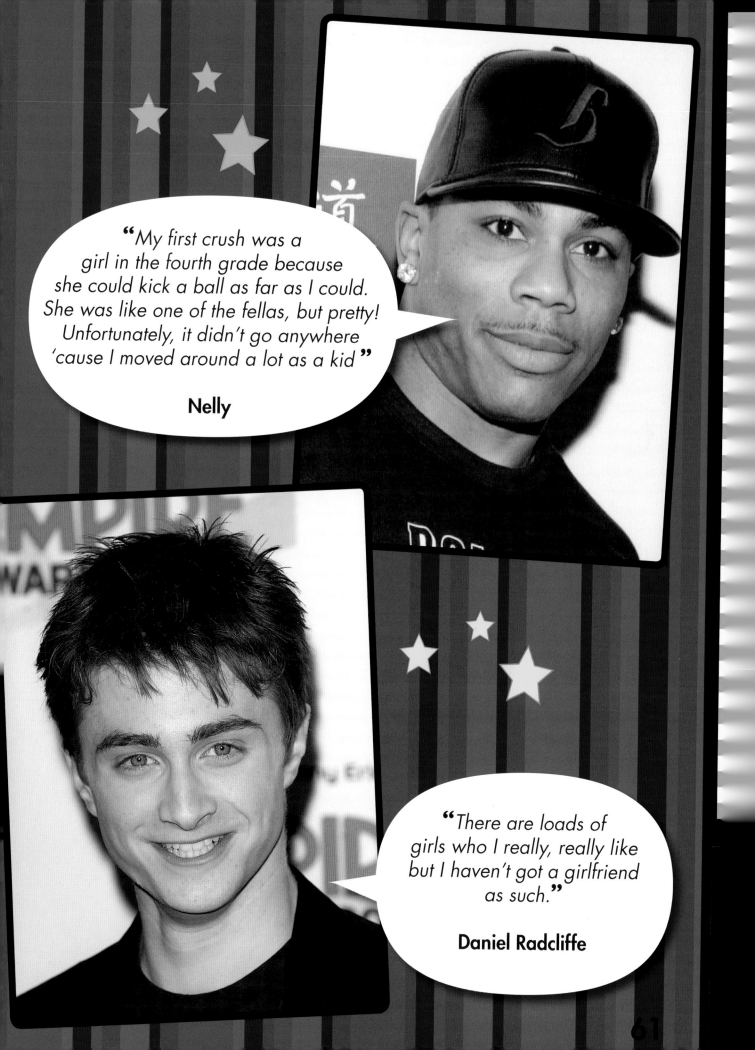

"My first crush was a girl in the fourth grade because she could kick a ball as far as I could. She was like one of the fellas, but pretty! Unfortunately, it didn't go anywhere 'cause I moved around a lot as a kid"

Nelly

"There are loads of girls who I really, really like but I haven't got a girlfriend as such."

Daniel Radcliffe

6

KEY TO HIS HEART

So you wanna score a date with your favourite hottie? Well psssstt, we've got the secret keys to their heart!

If Zac is your dream dude, then invite him over to watch *Moulin Rouge* – not only is it his favourite, it makes him cry, so get the tissues at the ready and offer him your shoulder!

You'll need to get your dancing shoes on to bag Usher. He loves nothing more than a girl who knows how to move on the dance floor!

Chris Brown loves it when a girl is interested in what he does, so to get to spend quality time with this crushable cutie, go listen to his last two albums, pronto!

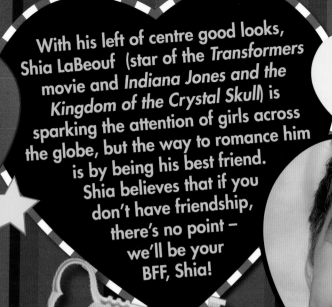

With his left of centre good looks, Shia LaBeouf (star of the *Transformers* movie and *Indiana Jones and the Kingdom of the Crystal Skull*) is sparking the attention of girls across the globe, but the way to romance him is by being his best friend. Shia believes that if you don't have friendship, there's no point – we'll be your BFF, Shia!

To make your crush fall for you, try this love spell

You will need

💜 *A red rose or rose petals* 💜 *A key* 💜 *30cm red ribbon*

1. On the night of the full moon – just before the hour of midnight – sit in your room.

2. Hold the rose and ribbon in your right hand.

3. Hold the key in your left hand and repeat:
   "The key to my heart is jumping, So (name of the person), take the plunge and get my heart pumping, for my heart is oozing love, And I don't want to be losing your love, So it shall be."

4. Take the key from your left hand, hang it on the red ribbon and wear it around your neck as you repeat the words again.

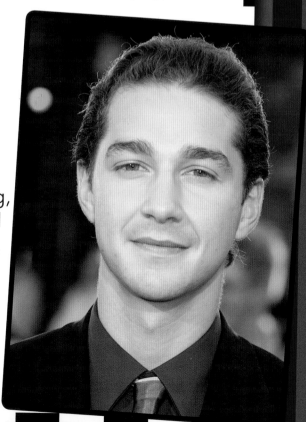

STAR STYLE

These girls get to hang out with some of our favourite celeb boys, we're not jealous, we just want to know their secret! We've been spying on four of the gals we'd love to be!

ASHLEY TISDALE

Serious Superstar: Ashley Tisdale
Age: 23
Where you've seen her: She plays Sharpay in *High School Musical* and Maddie in *The Suite Life of Zac and Cody*
Favourite Quote: "I totally love pink, it's just so girly!"
Style: She's glam-girl-tastic! She loves sequins and sparkles and loves nothing more than to work a red carpet outfit!

Why we heart her: Ashley's a true glamour puss and a twinkly superstar. Plus without her, *HSM* just wouldn't be the same!

Diva Detective: Emma Roberts (Julia Roberts niece)
Age: 17
Where you've seen her: She plays Addie in *Unfabulous* and glam supersleuth, *Nancy Drew!*
Favourite Quote: When I was at school we all dressed like twins!"
Style: She's girl-next-door without being frumpy. She matches cute off-the-shoulder tops with jeans – we love casual chic!

Why we heart her: Emma is far from unfabulous! She can sing, dance and she makes a totally dazzling detective! Keep your files up-to-date on this superstar.

MILEY CYRUS

Smiley Miley: Miley Cyrus

Age: 16

Where you've seen her: She's Hannah Montana of course!

Favourite Quote: "My dad says I could sing before I could talk, if that's possible!"

Style: Just like Hannah, Miley isn't afraid to be adventurous with her choice of outfits, she's not always right, but she has fun playing with her style and we love her for that!

Why we heart her: Miley's a multi-talented miss, who's magic on the microphone AND has an address book brimmin' with celeb bezzies! Plus, we so can't get enough of Hannah Montana!

EMMA WATSON

Stylish Starlet: Emma Watson
Age: 18
Where you've seen her: *Harry Potter* and *Ballet Shoes*
Favourite Quote: "I love fashion, it's how you show yourself to the world."
Style: This girl knows how to wear clothes and looks just as great in dress-down jeans and tee as she does wearing a couture dress to a film premiere – Em, we salute you!
Why we heart her: Emma was born to be a star with her dazzling sense of style and acting skills. But she hasn't let it go to her head – her feet are firmly on the ground. We're spellbound!

COULD YOU BE ZAC'S GIRL?

Just like his character Link Larkin in the movie *Hairspray*, Zac is deffo the ladies choice, but would he fall for you?

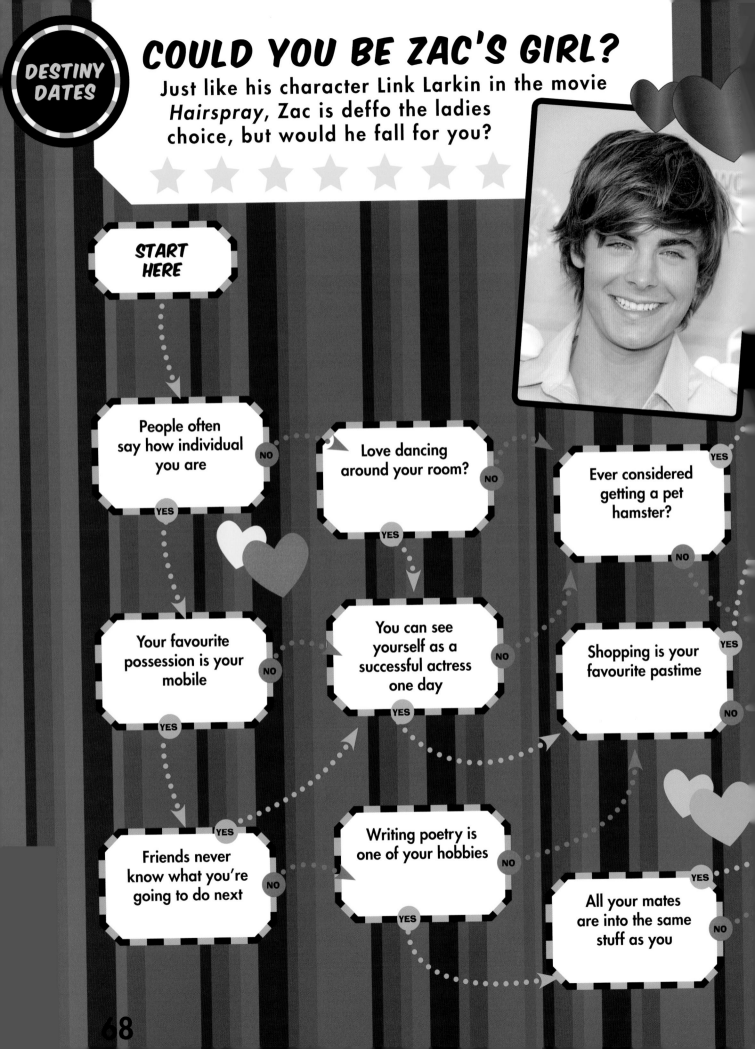

START HERE

People often say how individual you are
— NO
— YES

Love dancing around your room?
— NO
— YES

Ever considered getting a pet hamster?
— YES
— NO

Your favourite possession is your mobile
— NO
— YES

You can see yourself as a successful actress one day
— NO
— YES

Shopping is your favourite pastime
— YES
— NO

Friends never know what you're going to do next
— YES
— NO

Writing poetry is one of your hobbies
— NO
— YES

All your mates are into the same stuff as you
— YES
— NO

Do you sometimes play old 60s records?

NO

YES

Are you super organized?

NO

YES

Is black your favourite colour?

NO

YES

YES | NO

Coming up with crazy ideas is your speciality

You're Zac's girl

You love 60s music, you love acting and your favourite way to chill is to watch a movie – three of Zac's most favourite things! You've got a mellow, kind nature and approach life in a straightforward way. You'd definitely appeal to down-to-earth chilled out Zac – hurrah!

You're Troy's girl

You've got a wild streak, but it doesn't rule your life – Troy, Zac's character in *HSM* plays for The Wildcats and like you knows how to have fun, but takes things seriously when it's necessary, and your mates can always rely on you. Your cool mix of headstrong and sorted is a cert to grab a lad like Troy!

You're Link's girl

Creative and kooky that's you! Your quirky view of life is just like Tracy Turnblad's in the movie *Hairspray*, and Zac's character Link Larkin fell for her big time! We bet you customize your clothes and stand out in a crowd. If anyone called you normal, you'd take it as an insult!

ELEMENTAL BOYS
Find out which element you are and what secret it reveals about you and your celeb crush!

★ ★ ★ ★ ★ ★ ★ ★ ★

WATER

Star signs:
Cancer, Pisces, Scorpio

Water signs are sensitive and arty – but you can be a bit scatty and indecisive sometimes! You're an amazing friend, who always has time to listen – just make sure you give yourself, and your incredible creativity, enough time and attention.

You look pretty in:
Turquoise, White, Silver

Your perfect star boy is an Earth sign, think David Beckham and Jared Leto - he'll keep your feet on the ground when you're taken away on a wave of wistfulness!

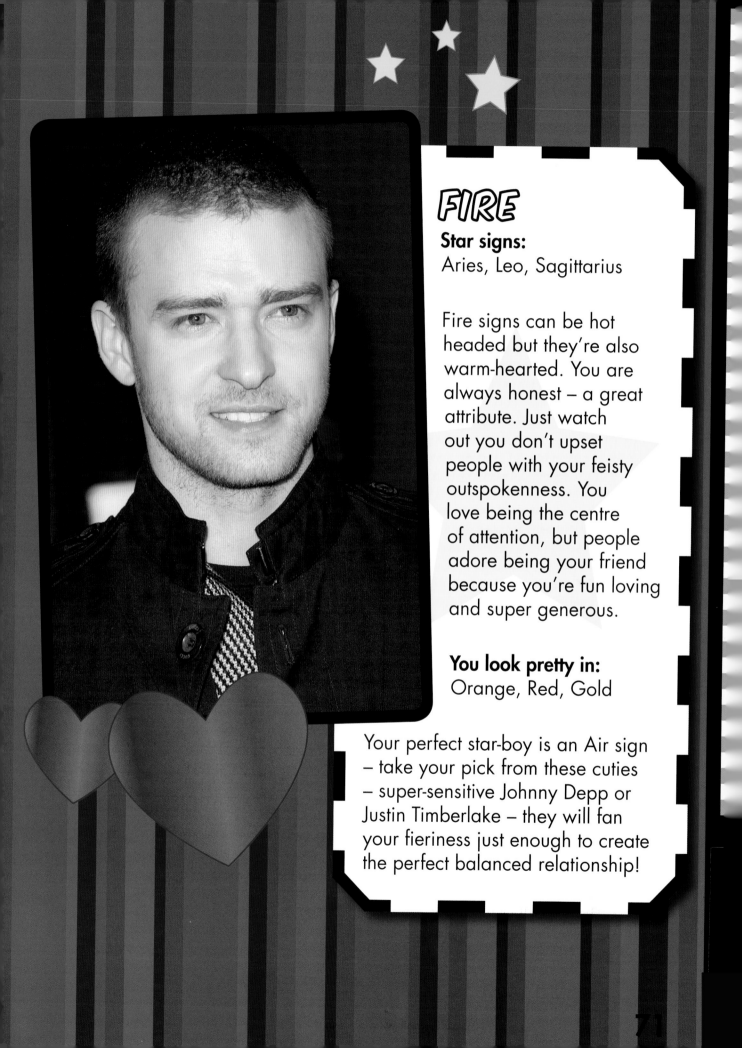

FIRE

Star signs:
Aries, Leo, Sagittarius

Fire signs can be hot headed but they're also warm-hearted. You are always honest – a great attribute. Just watch out you don't upset people with your feisty outspokenness. You love being the centre of attention, but people adore being your friend because you're fun loving and super generous.

You look pretty in:
Orange, Red, Gold

Your perfect star-boy is an Air sign – take your pick from these cuties – super-sensitive Johnny Depp or Justin Timberlake – they will fan your fieriness just enough to create the perfect balanced relationship!

EARTH

Star signs:
Taurus, Virgo, Capricorn

Earth signs always have
their feet on the ground
and don't like taking too
many risks. Just make sure
you're not too sensible
all the time – sometimes
it's fun to go out and be
a tiny bit spontaneous!
You're a caring,
supportive friend and
everyone knows they can
count on you.

You look pretty in:
Green, Yellow, Brown

Your perfect star-boy is
a water sign, your choices include
the dee-lish Ashton Kutcher, and
Harry Potter actor, Daniel Radcliffe
–they'll make sure your deepest
feelings come bubbling to the
surface.

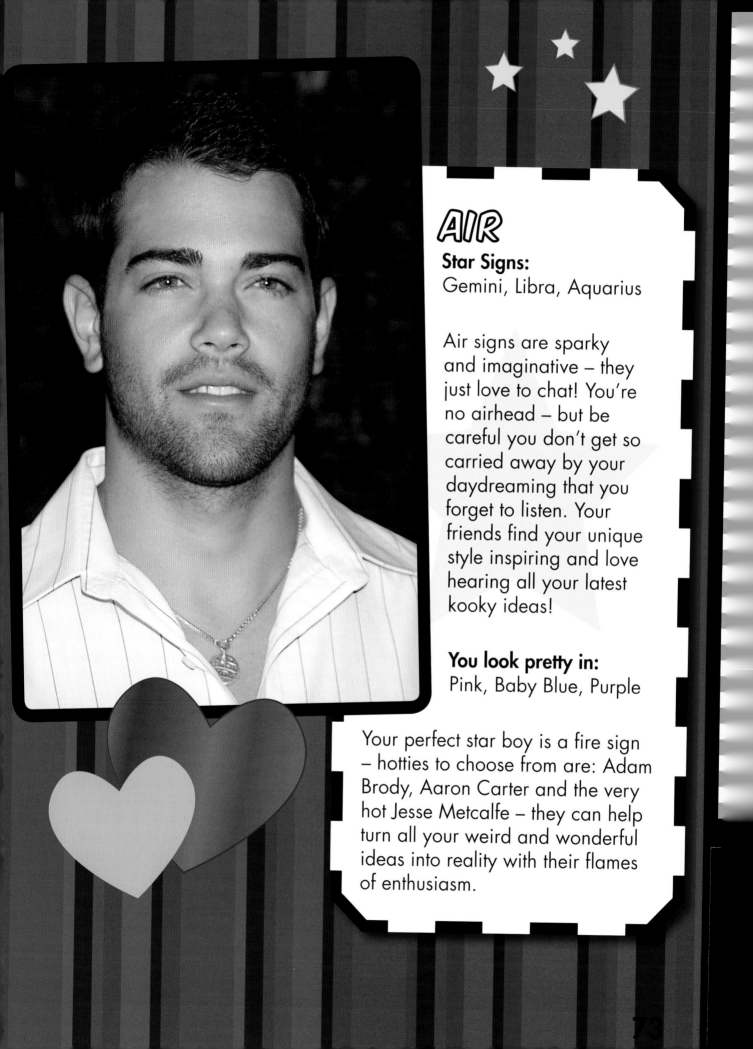

AIR

Star Signs:
Gemini, Libra, Aquarius

Air signs are sparky and imaginative – they just love to chat! You're no airhead – but be careful you don't get so carried away by your daydreaming that you forget to listen. Your friends find your unique style inspiring and love hearing all your latest kooky ideas!

You look pretty in:
Pink, Baby Blue, Purple

Your perfect star boy is a fire sign – hotties to choose from are: Adam Brody, Aaron Carter and the very hot Jesse Metcalfe – they can help turn all your weird and wonderful ideas into reality with their flames of enthusiasm.

DESTINY DATES

DESTINATION FAME GAME

Race your friends along the red carpet to mega stardom!

22.
CRINGE STOP!
Make a sign saying "Simon Cowell is hot!" and stick it on your bedroom door for one week!

21

20. Your limo driver runs over J-Lo's toes by accident and she's not impressed. **Go back two places.**

12.
CRINGE STOP!
It's time to be centre of attention. Stand on a chair and sing a song from *HSM* as loud as you can.

13. Uh-oh… Mary Kate and Ashley have both copied your haircut. **Go back five**

11

10. Your pet pooch gets into a bit of a fight with Paris Hilton's ferret – oh no! **Go back two.**

How to play:
Cut out the four celeb-girl counters and take one each.
Roll a dice to get started.
If you land on a cringe stop! You have to do exactly what it says (no excuses!)
Whoever makes it to the end is the A-list celeb!

1.
START

2. You're snapped smooching the gorgeous Orlie Bloom. **Go forward four spaces!**

23. Zac Efron asks if you wanna go ice skating with him. Like he even needed to ask! **Move on two spaces.**

24

25. YAY! You've survived the red carpet. **You're a true A-lister!**

19. You slip on an icy puddle, but Jake Gyllenhaal is passing and catches you! **Go forward two.**

18

17. CRINGE STOP! Give a big high five to the next person who comes in the room even if it's your Gran.

14. You bump into Jesse McCartney at a yoga class and go for a hot chocolate. **Go forward one.**

15

16. Corbin Bleu texts you asking for date. **Move on two spaces.**

9. Pete Wentz has sent you flowers! Sigh. **Move on two spaces.**

8

7. CRINGE STOP! Confess your most embarrassing crush to your mates Now, be honest!

6

3

4. You get so many letters of love from celeb admirers, you need your very own postman. **Move on two spaces.**

5. You spill Cola all over your designer dress at JT's after-show party. **Go back two spaces.**

DESTINY DATES

SUPERSTAR SECRETS!

How DO we know the following things? We aren't just a whiz with our celebrity crystal ball – we found out just what our top boys were most afraid of. Guess the answers!

★ ★ ★ ★ ★ ★ ★ ★ ★ ★

A. Even though he had to shoot scenes with giant spider, this cute boy-type is terrified of the eight-legged beasts!

B. This celeb won't negotiate with er…bathrooms! He's scared of getting trapped in a cubicle.

C. This hero beat his fear of heights to swing sky-high on screen.

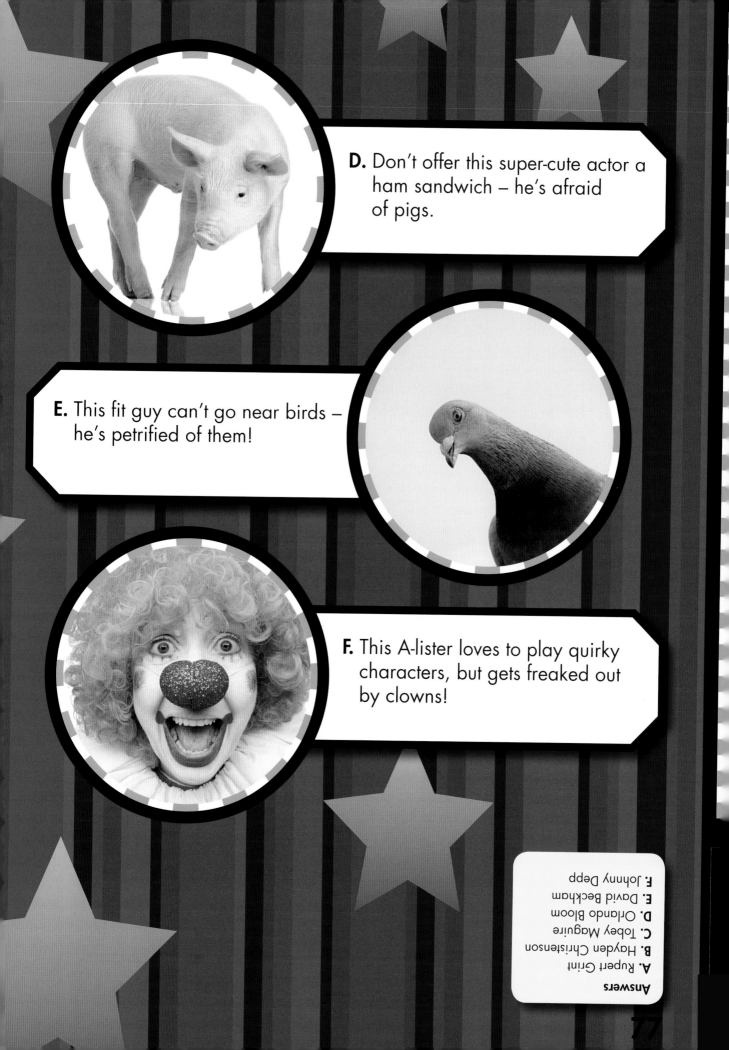

D. Don't offer this super-cute actor a ham sandwich – he's afraid of pigs.

E. This fit guy can't go near birds – he's petrified of them!

F. This A-lister loves to play quirky characters, but gets freaked out by clowns!

ORLANDO BLOOM

WALL CANDY

WELCOME TO
HOTSVILLE

Just imagine what a fantastic, fun-filled eye-candy place of wonder a town filled with *ALL* your adorable boy crushes would be? Where they all actually lived and worked next to each other? Well, we did too! So, forget The Holly-hood, welcome to Hotsville… and you don't have to catch a train or bus to get there either – because girl, you've just arrived!

Matt Damon – video arcade owner
This is a slightly self-indulgent pasttime for Matt as they're one of his favourite places to hang out!

Joaquín Phoenix – librarian.
He's got a touch of the super-geek about him and we think he'd look good in glasses…or anything really…

Jesse McCartney – physical trainer/ baseball coach
Jesse loves working out and would be the perfect coach – we're suddenly really interested in baseball

Josh Hartnett runs the local DVD/video store. He will be able to provide you with your movie fix as this is what he used to do before he became a famous celeb boy!

Ashton Kutcher & Jake Gyllenhaal – lifeguards at the local swimming pool
Two of the cutest boys in celeb-land in nothing but red shorts – yum! Ashton starred in the film, *The Guardian* with Kevin Costner and Jake used to be a real a beach lifeguard – we'd feel very safe in this dynamic duo's hands.

Milo Ventimiglia – restaurant owner/ chef. Not only is he good-enough-to-eat, he's a trained and accomplished cook – whip me up a *Heroes* sized treat, pronto!

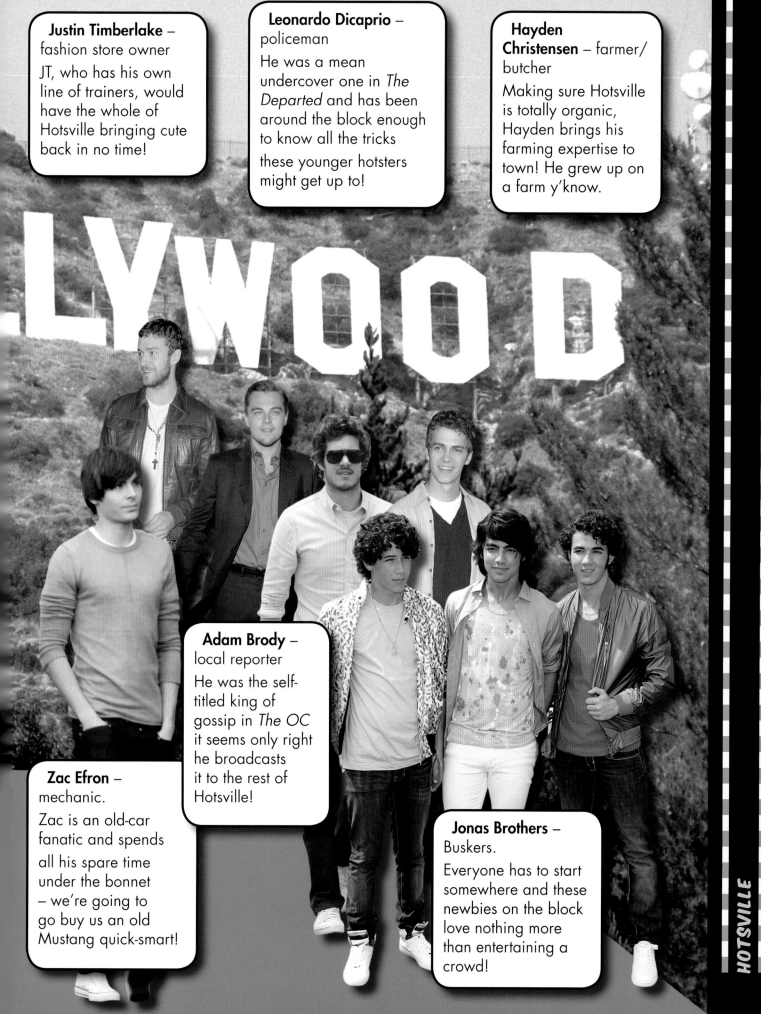

Justin Timberlake – fashion store owner JT, who has his own line of trainers, would have the whole of Hotsville bringing cute back in no time!

Leonardo Dicaprio – policeman
He was a mean undercover one in *The Departed* and has been around the block enough to know all the tricks these younger hotsters might get up to!

Hayden Christensen – farmer/butcher
Making sure Hotsville is totally organic, Hayden brings his farming expertise to town! He grew up on a farm y'know.

Adam Brody – local reporter
He was the self-titled king of gossip in *The OC* it seems only right he broadcasts it to the rest of Hotsville!

Zac Efron – mechanic.
Zac is an old-car fanatic and spends all his spare time under the bonnet – we're going to go buy us an old Mustang quick-smart!

Jonas Brothers – Buskers.
Everyone has to start somewhere and these newbies on the block love nothing more than entertaining a crowd!

MATE OR DATE?

Which of these favourite hotsters would be a cool mate or a fab date? You decide!

★ ★ ★ ★ ★ ★ ★ ★ ★ ★

NICK JONAS

☐ DATE

He loves to buy presents for people so as his date, we're thinking flowers and chocolates?!

You'll be guaranteed a sweet treat on your date as Nick loves ice-cream and he's okay with sharing it too – yay!

His favourite way to chill on a rainy day is to watch movies – ours too, Nick!

☐ MATE

He has an obsession with his socks – something you could deal with in a mate but not as a date.

He prefers texting to actually talking – which again is fine if you're buds, but you'd like a bit of talk time with a beau, right?

He likes to give his opinion on everything – that would get really annoying after a while.

SHIA LABEOUF

☐ DATE

He's a daredevil – on the set of *Indiana Jones and The Kingdom of The Crystal Skull*, he was given flying lessons in a helicopter – a date with him would definitely be an adventure!

He's multi-talented – not only is he an award-winning actor he plays the drums too!

He loves animals – he has two dogs called Brando and Rex and we love a boy that loves animals!

☐ MATE

Shia is an only child so may be a bit protective of you as a girlfriend.

He crushes on Mary-Kate Olsen.

He celebrates both Christmas and Hannukah and loves to have fun – this makes him the perfect party pal.

DANIEL RADCLIFFE

☐ DATE

Dan will be earning a reported $50 million total for the final two Harry movies – the popcorn's on him!

He's often mistaken for cutie Elijah Wood – two famous boyfriends for the price of one – hurrah!

He loves The Killers – we love a boy that loves to rock out and play air guitar with us!

☐ MATE

Dan has said on many occasions that his biggest challenge is girls. So to avoid any awkwardness friendship could be the way forward

Daniel can rotate his arm at a 360 degree angle – not so helpful on a date but as a mate he'll be able to reach those top shelf hand bags you need!

He loves his ipod more than life itself – you can hang out together and talk music while listening to an ear each – perfect bud time!

HOTSVILLE

WHAT'S YOUR PERFECT
CELEB PARTY?

Find out what bash and what boys get your vote...

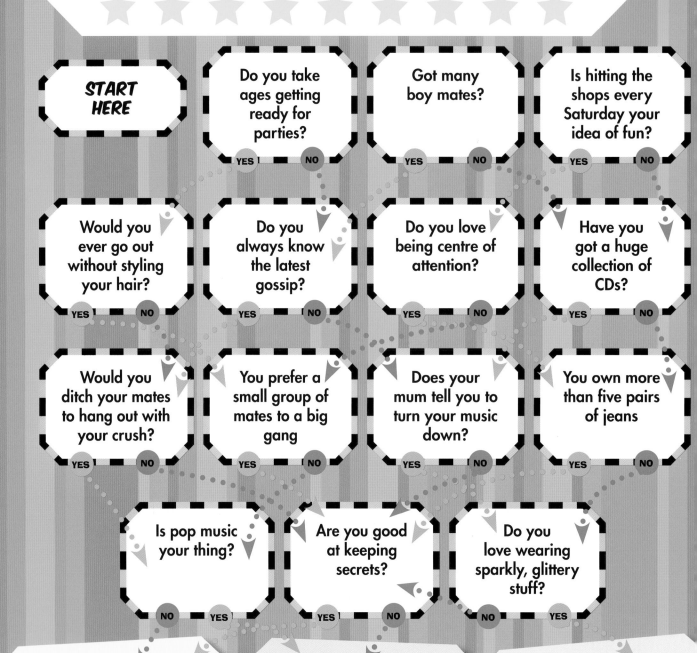

START HERE

Do you take ages getting ready for parties? YES | NO

Got many boy mates? YES | NO

Is hitting the shops every Saturday your idea of fun? YES | NO

Would you ever go out without styling your hair? YES | NO

Do you always know the latest gossip? YES | NO

Do you love being centre of attention? YES | NO

Have you got a huge collection of CDs? YES | NO

Would you ditch your mates to hang out with your crush? YES | NO

You prefer a small group of mates to a big gang YES | NO

Does your mum tell you to turn your music down? YES | NO

You own more than five pairs of jeans YES | NO

Is pop music your thing? NO | YES

Are you good at keeping secrets? YES | NO

Do you love wearing sparkly, glittery stuff? NO | YES

Rocker's Riot
You're a bit of a rock chick at heart, so you'd fit right in at a cool rock bash with the likes of Jonas Brothers and Simple Plan. Remember to wear your black eyeliner, ripped jeans and cute band tee – and don't forget to turn your music up really LOUD!

Celeb bash
A red-carpet event is perfect for you. You could walk with Johnny and Brad on either arm and text your gal-pals about all the latest star scandals. You'll then hit the dance floor at the after-show party to show off your amazing moves!

Girly get-together
A girly get-together with Miley, Vanessa and Ashley would be right up your street – it would be perfect for spilling secrets, catching up on who's crushing on who, swapping style tips and showing off your party outfit

DANIEL RADCLIFFE

WALL CANDY

THE HOLLYWOOD HOTSVILLE AWARDS

Forget the Golden Globes, wave goodbye to the MTV Music Awards and say goodbye to Oscar season, because there's a new awards ceremony hitting the glitz and glamour of the star-lined sidewalks of the Hottie Hometown.

It's the Hollywood Hotsville Awards!

The nominations for the totally Hottest Hotsville Hotties on the planet go to…

TOTAL HOTTIE

Total Hotties Award for Being the Most Huggable
Cody Linley cos.. he's well just…
AAAAAAHHHHH!

TOTAL HOTTIE

Total Hotties Award for the Best Hair
Corbin Bleu – he puts the "corrr" into Corbin - just look at why

TOTAL HOTTIE

Total Hotties Award for "Shhh – we've got a Secret Crush"
Rupert Grint for being the nerdy, quick-witted, surprisingly hot wizard in *Harry Potter*

TO HOT

Total Hotties Award for Most Likely to Have the Longest Career
Daniel Radcliffe – this boy can do no wrong – he jumps from movie screen, to TV to theatre in a flick of his wand and a swoosh of his broomstick!

TOTAL HOTTIE

Total Hotties Award for
Being the Most Musical
Justin Timberlake cos he makes
us cry a river and he's gorgeous
all the time!

TOTAL HOTTIE

Total Hotties Award for
Being the Class Clown
Lil' JJ for being a stand-up
comedian when he was small
and for never stop messing
around in class at school!

TOTAL HOTTIE

Total Hotties Award for
the Date Most Likely to Fly Away
Milo Ventimiglia for playing the
flying Peter Petrelli in *Heroes*
(Runner Up in this Category is
Chris Evans as Johnny Storm in
the *Fantastic Four*)

TOTAL HOTTIE

Total Hotties Award for
Looking Cooler, Hotter and
More Beautiful as You Get Old
Johnny Depp for effortlessly
jumping out of the screen as a
pure King of the Hotties
every time

TOTAL HOTTIE

Total Hotties Award for
the Freakiest Smile
Spencer Pratt – not on our list of
hotties because when he opens
his mouth you want to run and
hide – look!

COOL KIDS ON THE BLOCK

When you're a Hollywood Hottie hanging around on a Saturday afternoon (because filming has finished on your latest blockbuster or you've just laid down tracks on your new album), then it helps if you've got pals nearby to call on.

And that's exactly what the Disney crew do as they all live in the same area...the Holly-hood!

If you wanna be famous, then Toluca Lake in the San Fernando Valley, near north Hollywood, is the place to live. If you've got a spare $5 million dollars for your LA pad – or super-rich parentals – then book your flight today!

But, before you arrive, take a look at who your neighbours will be, where you'll be likely to bump into your crushes and what there is to do in the Holly-hood area nearby...

Recording
Vanessa and Ashley go to a secret **Santa Monica** recording studio, along with lots of the *HSM* crew, to record the movie soundtracks – la-la-la!

Living

Zac Efron, Vanessa Hudgens, Miley Cyrus and Ashley Tisdale all reside in super posh Toluca Lake. The Jonas Brothers live next door to Miley Cyrus and they are joined by other hot celebs in the area, such as Christina Aguilera, Hilary Duff, Kirsten Dunst, Jennifer Love Hewitt and Shia LaBeouf. This is one star-spangled neighbourhood!

Eating

Zac and Vanessa love to eat out, and who wouldn't wanna be seen out with Zac, right? So they chow down at:

California Pizza Kitchen – try their famous pizzas dripping with cheese at 6801 Hollywood Blvd., Sp. D2-225
Hollywood, CA 90028

Bobs Big Boy restaurant – get burgers and desserts, but if you go you have to try the famous BigBoy Sandwich at 5050 Wilshire Blvd , LA 90036

Patty's Diner – get a hearty breakfast (served all day) or tuck into any of this popular diner's yummy-scrummy meals at 10001 Riverside Dr Toluca Lake, CA 91602

Lola's – they love to get some quiet time in their own booth here in this funky restaurant and bar at: 945 North Fairfax Avenue Los Angeles, CA 90046, Mo's Fine Food in Woodland Hills at 20969 Ventura Blvd Woodland Hills, CA 91364
And any other Studio City restaurant…

Drinking

Coffee drinking is what celebs do best and celebs like Zac, Ashley and Nick Jonas are often spotted at the Coffee Bean & Tea Leaf which is a favourite hangout or for that all-important takeout coffee look – think **Mary-Kate Olsen**, head to: 10121 Riverside Drive, Toluca Lake CA, 91602
Pinkberry on 12044 1/2 Ventura Blvd. Studio City, CA 91604 is where you'll find the Jonas Brothers getting their healthy frozen yogurts and smoothies **– yum!**

Shopping

Urban Outfitters in Studio City is a favourite with all the stars, but Zac is a **HUGE** fan!

The Lisa Kline boutique is perfect for all girly necessities as Vanessa and Ashley will tell you as this is their main hang-out at 7207 Melrose Ave., Los Angeles, CA, also managing to fit in visits at: West Hollywood stores, Fred Segal, Ron Herman and Louis Vuitton

Exercise

These celeb-types love to keep in shape and Vanessa Hudgens and Ashley Tisdale (Ashnessa) go to pilates together at a fitness center in Encino, CA
While Zac and best friend Bubba Lewis, get their fitness on at the LA Fitness gym at 7021 Hollywood Blvd # 218, Los Angeles, CA
When Vanessa's not at the gym, she walks her pooch, Shadow, in Riverside Drive, while Lakeside Golf Club has lots to offer, with a more leisurely exercise routine for busy hotties like the Jonas Brothers.

TOP 5 HOTSVILLE HOTTIES

For each category, write down your personal top five!

★ ★ ★ ★ ★ ★ ★ ★ ★ ★ ★

MY TOP FIVE HOT BOYS I'D LIKE TO HANG OUT WITH.

....

....

....

....

....

MY TOP FIVE HOT BOYS WHO TOP THE CHARTS

....

....

....

....

....

MY TOP FIVE HOT BOYS WHO STEAL THE SCREEN IN EVERY SCENE...

....

....

....

....

MY TOP FIVE HOT BOYS WHO I'D SLOW-DANCE WITH...

....

....

....

....

....

MY TOP FIVE BOYS WHO ARE TOTALLY NOT WELCOME IN MY WORLD

....

....

....

....

....

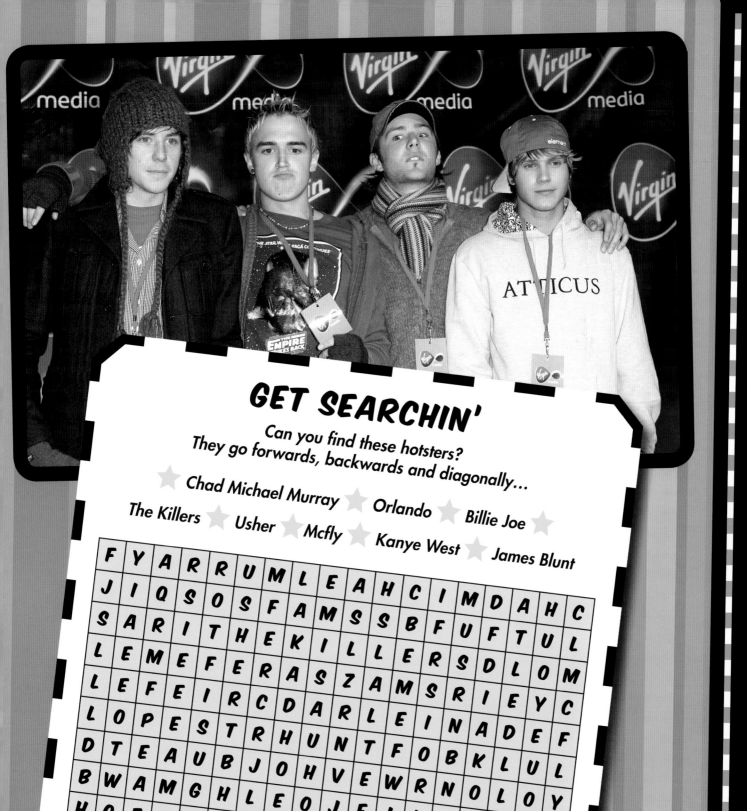

GET SEARCHIN'

Can you find these hotsters?
They go forwards, backwards and diagonally...

⭐ Chad Michael Murray ⭐ Orlando ⭐ Billie Joe ⭐
The Killers ⭐ Usher ⭐ Mcfly ⭐ Kanye West ⭐ James Blunt

F	Y	A	R	R	U	M	L	E	A	H	C	I	M	D	A	H	C
J	I	Q	S	O	S	F	A	M	S	S	B	F	U	F	T	U	L
S	A	R	I	T	H	E	K	I	L	L	E	R	S	D	L	O	M
L	E	M	E	F	E	R	A	S	Z	A	M	S	R	I	E	Y	C
L	E	F	E	I	R	C	D	A	R	L	E	I	N	A	D	E	F
L	O	P	E	S	T	R	H	U	N	T	F	O	B	K	L	U	L
D	T	E	A	U	B	J	O	H	V	E	W	R	N	O	L	O	Y
B	W	A	M	G	H	L	E	O	J	E	I	L	L	I	B	B	W
H	O	F	P	I	C	E	U	N	A	E	D	A	N	G	M	I	A
A	C	R	I	S	T	I	A	N	O	R	O	N	A	L	D	O	R
G	L	R	E	P	I	N	L	L	T	Y	D	D	U	G	U	B	T
K	A	N	Y	E	W	E	S	T	D	S	D	O	I	L	J	A	S

HOTSVILLE

CELEB DOKU
Their numbers are up!
Can you put these A-listers in their place?

Celeb Doku has two simple rules:

- Each column, each row and each box must contain each of the celebrities numbered 1 to 9

- Therefore, no column, row or box can contain two squares with the same celebrity

1. Josh Hartnett 2. Matthew Fox
3. Chris Brown 4. Zac Efron
5. Justin Timberlake 6. Johnny Depp
7. Milo – *Heroes* 8. Tobey Maguire
9. Ashton Kutcher

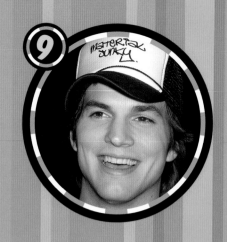
	4		2					
	7							2
	6			4	3	9		
			9	6				8
			3			4		
				1				3
1								
7			5					
9	5	3		8